COMMEMORATIVE EDITION

Sports Ill

Arnold

1929–2016

FRONT COVER:
Palmer competed at the 1963 World Series of Golf. *Photograph from Bettmann/Getty Images*

BACK COVER:
SI's Athletes of the Century fête in 1999 honored Arnie. *Photograph by Walter Iooss Jr.*

TITLE PAGE:
Palmer had powerfully strong hands. *Photograph by John Dominis/The LIFE Picture Collection/Getty Images*

THIS PAGE:
Private planes were Palmer's major indulgence. *Photograph by Michael O'Neill/Corbis/Getty Images*

CONTENTS

PARTS OF THIS EDITION WERE PUBLISHED PREVIOUSLY BY SPORTS ILLUSTRATED AND GOLF MAGAZINES

INTRODUCTION

The Essence Of Arnie

He loved people like he loved his next breath, and golf even more

BY RICK REILLY

From Golf.com
September 27, 2016

WHEN I HEARD Arnold Palmer died, I thought of my mom, Betty.

My mom was in love with Arnold Palmer. That was the only time I ever saw her sneak a glance at the Sylvania from the brownies she was making or the dishes she was rinsing—when Arnie was on the screen. Arnie was catnip in spikes to women. The way his hair wouldn't stay put and his pants wouldn't stay up, the ruggedness of his farm-boy arms and the why-go-inside tan, the tossed cigarette, the head-thrown-back laugh, the RCA-dog turn of the head as he watched his drive sail, the schoolboy grin and the sit-next-to-me eyes.

My mom would've liked him even better in person.

Here was Arnold Palmer: When he'd return his tournament courtesy car, he'd have washed it, gassed it and left four dozen balls in the front seat. When he'd borrow your club locker for the week, he'd leave you four shirts, four gloves and four more dozen balls. Arnold Palmer, one of the richest men in America, wrote handwritten thank you notes to the end.

Here was Arnold Palmer: When he'd see you, he'd grab your right hand and shake it, your right shoulder and hold it and say, "How the hell are ya?" Then the left hand might move up to behind your neck or maybe he'd pull you sideways and walk with it draped over your right shoulder, as though you were childhood chums. Ben Hogan was an icicle, Jack Nicklaus was a god, but Arnold Palmer was your poker buddy. The man went out of his way to make sure you knew he liked you.

Here was Arnold Palmer: He signed. My God, did he sign. He'd start in his office at about 7a.m. and sign for a good hour, every single morning, usually more. I know because that was the best time to interview him. I swear, he could sign his name while undergoing an appendectomy. And because he was so popular—the most popular golfer in history—and for so long (even into his 80s he would rank behind only Tiger Woods and Phil Mickelson in endorsements), he wound up signing his name more than any other athlete in history. What other superstar gave more ink than he got?

He was the perfect American to bring a dandruff-covered elitist British game called golf to the pipe fitters and the bus drivers and the brownie makers. He made it look fun. And joyful, and maddening, and utterly addictive. He would win heroically (seven behind with 18 to go at the 1960 U.S.Open at Cherry Hills) and lose catastrophically (seven ahead with nine to go at the '66 U.S. Open at Olympic Club), and never the twain seemed to meet. He never quit, never lagged and wouldn't lay up for all the coffee beans in Brazil.

Americans, in turn, loved him like their favorite son. At

the height of his popularity, when he was battling Fat Jack and his titanic drives and grim countenance, Arnie's Army was so devoted that there were reports of his soldiers actually letting Arnie's ball hit them to keep it from going over the green or into the rough. The red badge of love.

Arnie was real. He cried on TV more than Susan Lucci. One time, they led him into the pressroom at the 1994 U.S. Open at Oakmont—just a few 5-woods from his boyhood home in Latrobe, Pa. Arnie had announced it would be his last Open. He got to his chair, put the mic in front of him, started out O.K., and then just puddled. The words were in there, they just wouldn't come out. He got up, red-eyed, waved at everybody forlornly and started to walk out. And that's when some of the hardest-bitten men and women you'll ever meet—cynics all—stood as one and gave him a standing ovation.

AUGUSTA NATIONAL/GETTY IMAGES

I admired him so. He was a drinker but never seemed drunk. He was a winner but never seemed cocky. He was richer than many nations but came off like a guy who had a Christmas Club savings account. He had charisma pouring out of his ears, manners enough for entire towns, and swimming pools of testosterone. He flew his own planes, jiggered his own clubs and drank his vodka straight. He loved people like he loved his next breath and golf even more than that. Golf just got lucky.

SIGNATURE MOMENT At the 1964 Masters and everywhere else, Palmer was generous and tireless in giving autographs.

One time, at his Isleworth golf course in Orlando, I took $5 off him. He'd been talking about a par-5 you could reach in two by hooking a 3-wood over a lake that was a 250-yard carry if it was a foot.

"No way," I said.

"Bet?" he said.

"Five."

He just barely missed.

Of course, he was 68 then.

A Life In Pictures

On the course and off, Arnold Palmer displayed a remarkably winning way

JOHN DOMINIS/THE LIFE PICTURE COLLECTION/GETTY IMAGES

BEHIND THEIR MAN
Palmer enjoyed a great connection with his fans, and nowhere more so than at Augusta National, where Arnie's Army watched as he lined up a putt on his way to victory in 1962.

BETTMANN/GETTY IMAGES

"Arnold always had my back, and I had his. He was the king of our sport and always will be."

JACK NICKLAUS

TAKING ON WATER
Palmer's aggressive style of play sometimes led to trouble, as it did at the 1964 Bing Crosby Pro-Am in Pebble Beach.

ARCHIVE PHOTOS/GETTY IMAGES

"To me he was simply a dear friend for more than 60 years. I will miss him terribly."

GARY PLAYER

EASY DOES IT
Palmer relaxes in between shots during a tournament in 1961, when he was the Tour's scoring leader and finished second on the money list.

"I knew I could always call him for advice. I'm forever grateful for his friendship."

TIGER WOODS

DOZIER MOBLEY/AP

THE HOME TEAM
Palmer enjoys domestic life in Latrobe, Pa., with wife Winnie, daughter Amy, dog Thunder and pony Zorro.

LEADING SCOR
HOLE Prev 1 2 3 4 5 6 7 8 9
PAR Score 4 5 4 3 4 3 4 5 4
A PALMER 10 10 10 10 11 10 10 11 11 11
MARR 4 4 5 6 6 6 6 6 7 7
BUTLER 3 3 4 5 5 5 4 4 3 2
FERRIER 3 3 4 5 4 3 3 3 3 3
NICKLAUS 1 1 2 2 2 1 1 2 2 3
HOGAN 1 2 3 2 2 2 3 3 2 1

AUGUSTA NATIONAL/GETTY IMAGES

"Every player, me included, should thank you for what you brought to our great game."

GREG NORMAN

FANTASTIC FINISH The scoreboard tells the story as Palmer birdied the 18th and roared to his fourth Masters title, in 1964, by his largest margin of victory in that tournament.

BRIAN MORGAN/GETTY IMAGES

"I liked the game of golf when I met him. He made me love it."

JUSTIN TIMBERLAKE

LOFTY POSITION
On his list of passions, flying was not far behind golf, and after taking his first lessons in 1956, he continued piloting his own plane until 2011.

“Arnold Palmer had swagger before we had a name for it. . . . [He] was the American Dream come to life.”

BARACK OBAMA

BOB MARTIN

REFLECTION TIME The Army once again lined the course at Augusta as Arnie played in his final Masters in 2004, here competing in Wednesday's Par 3 Contest.

Titleist

A King In Full

A rare mix of warmth and bravado made Arnold Palmer his sport's most beloved figure

BY MICHAEL BAMBERGER

FLYBOY CHARM
Palmer, who preferred to wing his way from tournament to tournament, said that if he weren't a golfer, he would have been a professional pilot.

JOHN DOMINIS/TIME LIFE PICTURES/GETTY IMAGES

ARNOLD PALMER, who died on Sept. 25 at age 87, led an American life that will never be duplicated, so rooted was it in a lost time and a place and the sui generis composition of the man. The golf legend won his last major championship in 1964 and his last PGA Tour event in '73, but in the decades that followed, his status only grew. He had a knack for making people feel better about themselves and about their prospects. As a player, he allowed his fans to join him in his unbridled assertiveness. He created a vicarious thrill like no player before him and none since. When his skills faded and his hair turned silver and then white, he exuded true grandfatherly warmth. For these and other reasons, he was not only the most beloved figure ever to play golf but also the rare golfer who was able to transcend a niche sport and become an international figure.

At the 2016 Masters, Palmer attended the festivities but did not hit a ceremonial opening tee shot alongside his friends Jack Nicklaus and Gary Player—the trio was once marketed as the Big Three—and Nicklaus spoke about Palmer with notable sadness, already perhaps anticipating last week's news. In June, at the U.S. Open at Oakmont, 40 miles from Palmer's hometown of Latrobe, Pa., players and commentators paid

From Sports Illustrated, October 3, 2016

Chi Chi Rodriguez said, "Every touring pro should bow down and pray to Arnold Palmer."

tribute to the man known as the King, a nickname he said in a memoir being published in October 2016 that he was never comfortable with. All of golf has been preparing itself for Palmer's death, which for millions of players around the world was almost like losing a parent. For decades, Chi Chi Rodriguez preached this message: "Every touring pro should bow down and pray to Arnold Palmer, for what he did for golf."

In the late 1950s and early '60s, Palmer, by virtue of his spectacular wins and losses, made golf a sport that enjoyed broad popularity on TV. All he had to do was contend, and he often did. It has been said that Palmer sold a million color TVs—nobody wanted to watch him perform his magic in black-and-white, not the man of the house, nor the lady of the house. Yes, the terms are old-fashioned: Palmer connected with conservative Middle America in ways that made him the envy of various presidents, Republicans in particular. He had an especially close relationship with Dwight Eisenhower.

Palmer was an odd sort of matinee idol. He had a rugged, regular-guy handsomeness—more out of the John Wayne school than anything else—but he had a physicality that drew both men and women to him. Over the decades he became fantastically rich, worth hundreds of millions of dollars. He was a child of the Depression and the proud son of working-class parents, and he essentially lived a modest life, except for his penchant for private planes. Palmer was an accomplished pilot who at one point circumnavigated the globe in a particular class of plane faster than anyone had. In his everyday lunchtime grillroom conversation, he spoke of his flying adventures with the same enthusiasm he spoke of golf, which is saying something. The world has most likely never seen anybody who loved golf more than Palmer did. He played or hit balls almost every day. His late first wife, Winnie, used to say that her husband would not last long if he could no longer fly his own plane or hit balls. With great reluctance Palmer gave up his pilot's license in 2011, and he was hitting balls until close to his death.

Palmer didn't have the quick wit of, say, Muhammad Ali, but he did have a directness that endeared him to millions of people. Like a contemporary, Walter Cronkite, he was consistent, reliable and trustworthy. Asked how he made a 12 on a hole, Palmer said, "I missed the 15-footer for 11."

He was the first tour professional with his own raucous gallery. The original members of Arnie's Army were GIs from Camp Gordon in Augusta, Ga., and Palmer was at ease with the enlisted men, knocking

BETTMANN/GETTY IMAGES

IN HIS BLOOD
The son of a club pro, Palmer was swinging a club at age six (above); he turned pro soon after winning the U.S. Amateur (left) in 1954, at age 24.

back cold ones on those occasions when he and they landed at the same bar. For some years in the 1950s and '60s, Palmer was a smoker, a scotch-and-steak man, a night owl, but the protective press of his era never showed him that way. People who followed the game closely knew. He never pretended to be something other than what he was. Among other things, he was a college dropout (Wake Forest), an uninspired paint salesman (his job before turning pro at age 25) and a man capable of breathtaking impetuousness, on a Sunday afternoon with a title in the balance and in his private life too. He met Winnie Walzer, a 19-year-old college student, at an amateur event on a Tuesday in September '54 and proposed to her that Saturday night. "Her dad hated my ass," Palmer once said. "He said, 'You're going to marry a golf pro?' "

AUGUSTA NATIONAL/GETTY IMAGES

They were married from 1954 until Winnie's death in '99. The Winnie Palmer Hospital for Women and Babies in Orlando is a world-class center for neonatal care. The couple had two children, Amy and Peggy, who were largely shielded from the spotlight. Palmer won 62 events on the PGA Tour (he is fifth on the all-time list) and 10 more times on the Champions tour. In Palmer's 50s and early 60s, when he was playing the senior tour, that circuit enjoyed its greatest popularity. He won one U.S. Open, in 1960, two British Opens (1961 and '62) and four Masters titles (1958, '60, '62 and '64). He never won a PGA Championship, the PGA of America's flagship event, and although he was a longtime member of the organization, as was his father before him, he had various enduring frustrations with the entity. He believed that the golf body at first discriminated against his father, Deacon, the club pro at Latrobe Country Club, because he had difficulty walking as a result of childhood polio. Arnold also resented the fact that for the first six months of his professional career, he, like all rookies then, was serving an apprenticeship that prevented him from cashing checks he made from Tour events. Palmer had a wide stubborn streak and a long memory.

IKE LIKES ARNIE President Dwight Eisenhower and Augusta National chair Clifford Roberts laugh with Palmer at the Masters in the 1950s.

LIKE RONALD REAGAN and Warren Buffett, Palmer had a knack for reducing complex things to their essence. As a golfer he belonged to the see-ball, hit-ball school, and in his prime he drove it long and straight and putted as well as anybody. His swing had a slashing, muscular quality to it—there was nothing country club about his action—and that added to his popularity. He was the opposite of Ben Hogan in almost every way, and he succeeded Hogan as the best-known American golfer. The two men never enjoyed much of a rapport. Palmer once said, "He never called me anything except fella."

Palmer's ascendance came in 1960, at age 30, when he hit one of the most famous shots in history, driving the 346-yard par-4 1st hole in the final round of the U.S. Open at Cherry Hills outside Denver. That shot set up a two-putt birdie, gave birth to the Palmer Charge and was the first blow in a final-round 65 that allowed Palmer to surge from behind and win by two over Nicklaus and four over Hogan. Palmer spent the rest of his life reviewing the costs of that win, which he believed contributed to the ultimate futility of his efforts to win a second U.S. Open

THE BIG THREE
When Gary Player (left) and Jack Nicklaus arrived to challenge Palmer for his throne, it marked the beginning of tremendous competition, friendship—and television.

despite being in contention many times. He started to dial back the aggressiveness that had made him so dangerous. He revered what he called "our national championship." He regarded that Open win as the most significant of his career, in part because of how much his father valued it. When he started playing the British Open in 1960, Palmer revived interest in that championship at a time when many U.S. professionals couldn't be bothered with making the trip.

But it was his play at Augusta National, both brilliant and bone-headed, that defined his career. When he was approached to become a dues-paying member of the club in 1999, the first Tour professional to have the honor bestowed on him, the invitation struck a deep chord in him. He was the winner of the '54 U.S. Amateur, and the approval of the sophisticated, well-bred men who ran the USGA and populated the membership rolls at Augusta National meant more to him than he cared to let on. But the truth was that those men were far more in awe of Palmer than he was of them. As a businessman, they had nothing on him. Most notably, in '95 he cofounded Golf Channel.

Palmer is on the Mount Rushmore of American sportsmen. In 1960 he won the Masters and the U.S. Open and was named SPORTS ILLUSTRATED's Sportsman of the Year. A golfer—a golfer!—was now talked about as not only an athlete, but also one who could be discussed in the same breath as Mickey Mantle and Cassius Clay and Frank Gifford. American golf had its first working-class hero, and the sport would never be the same.

Palmer signed the cover of that Sportsman issue thousands of times in his flowing script. There cannot be anybody anywhere who has signed more autographs than Arnold Palmer.

In his later years, the ceremonial opening tee shot at the Masters helped keep Palmer in the public eye. There's a silver replica of the Augusta National clubhouse at the front door of his Latrobe office and another at the SpringHill Suites in Latrobe, a hotel Palmer owned that's located on Arnold Palmer Drive. Palmer lost three U.S. Opens in playoffs, and in his mind he should have won yet another three. Even though he won his last major in 1964, Palmer felt, on a technical level, that he played his best golf between '65 and '73. He was actually much more consistent than most people realize, and he won at least one Tour event every year from '55 through '71.

ROOT AROUND the soul of any professional golfer, and you'll find something melancholic. Fans remember Palmer tossing victory balls and flinging visors like they were Frisbees. Those photos were lodged in Palmer's mind too, but he remembered just as well the ones that got away. He revisited these events without bitterness but with genuine regret. Hearing him talk about these tournaments made him all the more real. He had a way of creating intimacy. Friends, relatives and employees were intensely loyal to him.

Unlike almost every other great champion, Palmer found joy in the game even after age started eroding his skills. He liked being in public, he liked being with the boys and he liked the challenge of trying to improve. He liked golf on every stage. One day when he was in his 70s, Palmer was playing a par-3 course in the California desert. Early on he found himself one down to a duffer, but then he started to turn the match around. He shook his club and yelled joyfully, "I got you now!"

Palmer wrote more golf books (10) than Dan Jenkins, designed or remodeled more courses (about 300) than Pete Dye and sponsored more products than Dale Earnhardt and Dale Jr. together. He drove a tractor for Pennzoil, ran through airports with O.J. Simpson for Hertz and appeared in an Electronic Arts video game with Tiger Woods. A hundred other deals could be added to that list. He appeared to be at once a conformist and a maverick, and people found that combination irresistible. He could be a Harvard Business School case study for the athlete as celebrity endorser and businessman. He paved the way for Jean-Claude Killy, Jackie Stewart, Michael Jordan, Phil Mickelson, Woods and many others.

Palmer was not close to Woods but was deeply impressed by his talent, and the two played together a handful of times. He occasionally watched Woods work on the driving range with Woods's father, Earl, at Isleworth, a massive Orlando real estate development in which Palmer was an early investor. He once said that Tiger's relationship with Earl reminded him of his own relationship with Deacon. Both fathers taught the importance of discipline and practice. Both instilled in their sons a competitive hunger bordering on voraciousness.

Palmer's longtime agent, Alastair Johnston, recruited Woods to IMG. Palmer himself had a long association with Mark McCormack, the founder of IMG and the man who invented the Big Three. Nicklaus, the Golden Bear, was a country-club kid and a plodder. Player, the Black Knight, was a globe-trotting overachiever with movie-star looks. Palmer was simply the King. In the 1960s, he gave the men's line at Sears a stamp of credibility, and he made cigarette smoking look cool. Later, he became a public face of an antismoking campaign. Palmer, a prostate cancer survivor in his late 60s, also made public service announcements about the importance of regular prostate exams.

Palmer played quickly, drove the ball long and straight and, with his inimitable knock-kneed, wristy stroke, could run the table with his putter. He was not one to sit around and hyperanalyze swing positions or the meaning of life. Asked about life regrets, Palmer once said, "I wish I would have tried putting left-hand low."

BETTMANN/GETTY IMAGES

MAN AND WIFE
In 1954 Palmer proposed to Winnie, then 19 years old, just four days after they first met, and they remained married for 44 years, until her death from cancer in 1999.

ARNOLD PALMER'S legacy is vast. He was part-owner of Bay Hill Club and Lodge, where a PGA Tour event bearing his name is played every March. He was an owner of the Pebble Beach Golf Links. Arnold Palmer was amused and a little embarrassed by the ubiquity of the beverage that bears his name, a lemonade–iced tea drink he is credited with inventing. There's a hospital named for him in Orlando and an airport named for him in Latrobe.

Palmer had six grandchildren and nine great-grandchildren. He married for a second time, in 2005, to Kit Gawthrop. He and Kit lived across the street from Latrobe Country Club, where his father had eventually become the head professional and his mother kept the books. Arnold bought the club in 1971. His home in Latrobe was a modern, boxy, comfortable mountain design, not some showpiece, and his prized possession in it was a landscape painting given to him by its artist, Dwight Eisenhower.

Palmer's official residence was a condo at Bay Hill, but Latrobe was the center of his universe. At Bay Hill he converted the garage into a workshop, and in it he spent many happy hours, bending clubs and chewing the fat with friends including former Tour player Dow Finsterwald; Palmer's longtime right-hand man, Doc Giffin; and various pilots and course superintendents who were both employees and friends. There was a small refrigerator in the workshop, and at 5 p.m. sharp, the first beers came out. In Latrobe, a massive barn served as a depository for 60 years of Palmer memorabilia, overseen by his younger brother, Jerry, who previously served as the general manager at Latrobe Country Club. He is also survived by two sisters, Lois Jean Tilley and Sandy Sarni.

Arnold Daniel Palmer—Arnie to most everyone—was a man of his generation. He insisted that men remove their hats upon entering the various clubhouses under his watch and was a big believer in the benefits of the firm handshake. He often said that the secret to his success as a golfer was the firm grip his father taught him as a child, just a few years after the great crash. He never changed his grip, he never changed his swing, he never changed his personality.

The New York Times columnist Dave Anderson once wrote that nobody could enjoy being who he or she is more than Arnold Palmer enjoys being Arnold Palmer. That observation got to the heart of the man and the matter. Palmer lived a full life and got millions of others to believe they could do the same.

HOUSE OF STICKS
Palmer, shown in 2007, had a collection of golf clubs that numbered more than 10,000.

KEVIN LORENZI/BLOOMBERG/GETTY IMAGES

Prime Time

JAMES DRAKE

Palmer

Arnie's success in golf's majors delivered the kind of excitement that made him a star

COMMANDING AN ARMY
"Masters galleries regard him as a chosen son," wrote Alfred Wright in SI after Palmer won at Augusta National for the fourth time, in 1964.

LEADING MEN
Palmer's duels with Jack Nicklaus in the early Masters tournaments—here Jack's the valet in '64—helped elevate both players, and also their sport.

THE MASTERS

The Green Giant

Whether he was winning, almost winning or simply embodying the joy of sport, Palmer had a long starring run at Augusta National

BY JOHN GARRITY

ARNOLD PALMER was born on April 6, 1958, on the back nine of Augusta National Golf Club. The midwife was Frank Chirkinian, a raucously profane television director sitting in a truck in the pines. As with any healthy delivery, Chirkinian saw Palmer's head first, then his shoulders and muscular arms, then his narrow hips as he crested a hill on the 15th fairway—all on a bank of black-and-white monitors. When Palmer, sizing up his approach shot, hitched up his pants and flipped aside his cigarette, the birth was complete. "The cameras capture the essence of a person," Chirkinian said years later. "They either love you or hate you, and they loved Arnold."

When Palmer teed it up for his 50th and final Masters in 2004, the cameras stalked him as they have stalked no other 74-year-old athlete in history. To watch Palmer go around Amen Corner is to make an archetypal connection.

MARVIN E. NEWMAN

FROM SPORTS ILLUSTRATED, APRIL 6, 2004

UPS AND DOWNS
If you were looking to root for the sure but steady type, best go somewhere else—even Palmer's triumphs included dips on the roller coaster, as with this chip at the 1960 Masters or a missed putt (right) at the '62 event, both tournaments he won.

AUGUSTA NATIONAL/GETTY IMAGES

It's Brando on a motorcycle. It's Armstrong on the moon. It's MacArthur wading ashore in the Philippines. "The Masters is Arnie's stage," longtime friend Howdy Giles said recently. "That's where he really shines."

Palmer won the Masters four times between 1958 and '64, and when he wasn't winning it, he was losing it. That is to say, he was Chirkinian's leading man whatever the outcome. Palmer finished third in '59, two strokes behind Art Wall, but housewives came out of their kitchens and stared over their husbands' heads at the monochrome majesty of Arnie, the son of a golf pro and greenkeeper from Latrobe, Pa. Two years later he lost his concentration on the final hole on Sunday, made double bogey and handed Gary Player his first Masters title. Golf fans of a certain age remember that collapse better than they remember details of their own weddings.

"I suppose I appreciated Augusta more than anyone," Palmer says, trying to explain why his identification with the Masters is stronger than that of any other player, even

UNDERWOOD ARCHIVES/GETTY IMAGES

"Palmer's connection to the fans—his Army—gave him an edge wherever he played but never more so than at Augusta National."

six-time champion Jack Nicklaus. "I was a golf pro's son, and the finances were tough when I was growing up. I was raised by my father to strive for high standards, and everything at Augusta was on such a high standard. There was no other golf tournament like it." On top of this blue-collar striving, Palmer had a need to prove that he belonged. He was hurt deeply when, in the locker room at the 1958 Masters, he overheard Ben Hogan ask another player, "How the hell did Palmer get an invitation to the Masters?"

Palmer could have confronted Hogan. Instead, he went out and won the tournament. That first victory, by a stroke over Doug Ford and Fred Hawkins, earned Palmer $11,250 (about $94,000 in 2016 dollars). More important, it gave Arnie a seat at the annual Masters champions' dinner, where he could exult in the practiced banter and storytelling of men like Claude Harmon, Byron Nelson, Gene Sarazen, Horton Smith, Sam Snead and Craig Wood. "That was a thrill for me," Palmer says of his acceptance by the past champions. "I was one of them."

Palmer's 50 Masters weeks add up to nearly a year of his life. His memories are necessarily partitioned; something that happened 30 years ago at Augusta may be more clearly recalled than a recent incident at a less meaningful place. The "year" began in April 1955, when Palmer, a pro for only five months, and his bride, Winnie, rolled into Augusta in a coral-pink Ford, towing a 19-foot trailer. (He tied for 10th that week, earning $696.) The following year the Palmers shared a Fort Gordon BOQ—Bachelor Officers' Quarters—with Dow Finsterwald and his wife, Linda. ("That turned out to be totally unacceptable," Finsterwald recalls with a smile. "My wife always described it as a barracks.") For the next seven years the Palmers spent Masters week in the Richmond Hotel, and it was during this short span that Palmer rose from golf serfdom to unchallenged status as the King, winning three Masters, a U.S. Open and two British Opens.

In week 10 of our Augustan year the Palmers rented a house on Aumond Road, and Arnie won his fourth and final Masters, burying Nicklaus and Dave Marr by six strokes. Walking up the 18th fairway on Sunday, Palmer turned to his pal Marr, who was still fighting for second, and asked if there was anything he could do to help. "Yeah," Marr said. "Make a 12."

Because the defending champion presents the winner with the green jacket after the Masters, Palmer's string of appearances at the ceremony reached seven that year. It would end at a record eight the following year, 1965, when Arnie played valet to Nicklaus for the second time.

FOR THE 50TH TIME
Palmer, who attracted legions of adoring fans long after his days of contending had passed, crossed the Hogan Bridge as he played in his 50th and final Masters in 2004, though he returned to Augusta National as the tournament's honorary starter from 2007 to '15.

AMY SANCETTA/AP

By then, Palmer's weeks at Augusta had settled into a rhythm that would prevail for four more decades. The champions' dinner on Tuesday night was always the highlight, but the Palmers entertained friends and family the rest of the week, either at the club, the house or a restaurant. When his playing schedule allowed, Arnie took lunch with friends under one of the green-and-white umbrellas on the Augusta National terrace. The chicken sandwich with Durkee's sauce was, in his words, "a particular fetish."

To fill the hours before an afternoon tee time, Palmer used to drive out to a retail golf shop near the Augusta airport and work on clubs with the proprietor, retired Army colonel Bernie Porter. "It was something to do to occupy the time, and it didn't take a lot of energy," Palmer recalls. "Winnie always insisted that I rest more, but that was tough for me. I needed to fix a club or fool around with the guys and listen to the B.S." In the 1970s Palmer's Augusta landlord, TV ad salesman Bert Harbin, installed a workbench in his garage so Palmer could tinker whenever he wanted. Says Harbin, "If he teed off in the afternoon, there would be 20 of us out there watching him fiddle with his clubs."

Palmer was the most unsolitary of men, and he took his gregariousness to the course. He waved to strangers. He veered to the ropes for a quick word with friends. He made the sunburned spectators in the uppermost row of the 13th-hole grandstand believe that he was playing for them. "He always seemed to be able to make eye contact," says Finsterwald. Palmer's connection to the fans—his Army, in the vernacular of the day—gave him an edge wherever he played but never more so than at Augusta National. In 1962 Player led Palmer by three and Finsterwald by six through nine holes of a Monday playoff that Palmer admitted he was "damn lucky to have made," as erratically as he had played on Sunday. "We've got to do something to make a match of this," Palmer told Finsterwald.

Well, sure. Palmer birdied four of the next five holes, made his fans delirious and wound up winning by three.

That was an eon ago in terms of sports, where records are broken every other week and new heroes pop up like hybrid corn in a heavily fertilized field. The Masters has changed. The crowds are bigger, the greens are faster, and the azaleas bloom at the command of heating elements buried in the soil.

But Palmer standing on the 1st tee in 2004 was a rebirth. "What some players don't seem to quite grasp," he wrote in a 1999 autobiography, "is that golf's enormous success can be attributed almost entirely to the fact that it hasn't changed much in a world in which values are constantly shifting or, as some believe, eroding."

Chirkinian's cameras loved Palmer, all right, but there was more to it than the hitch of the pants and the flip of the cigarette. The man striding up the hill into America's living rooms knew exactly who he was and exactly what he wanted, and by some wonderful stroke of luck it was exactly what America wanted too.

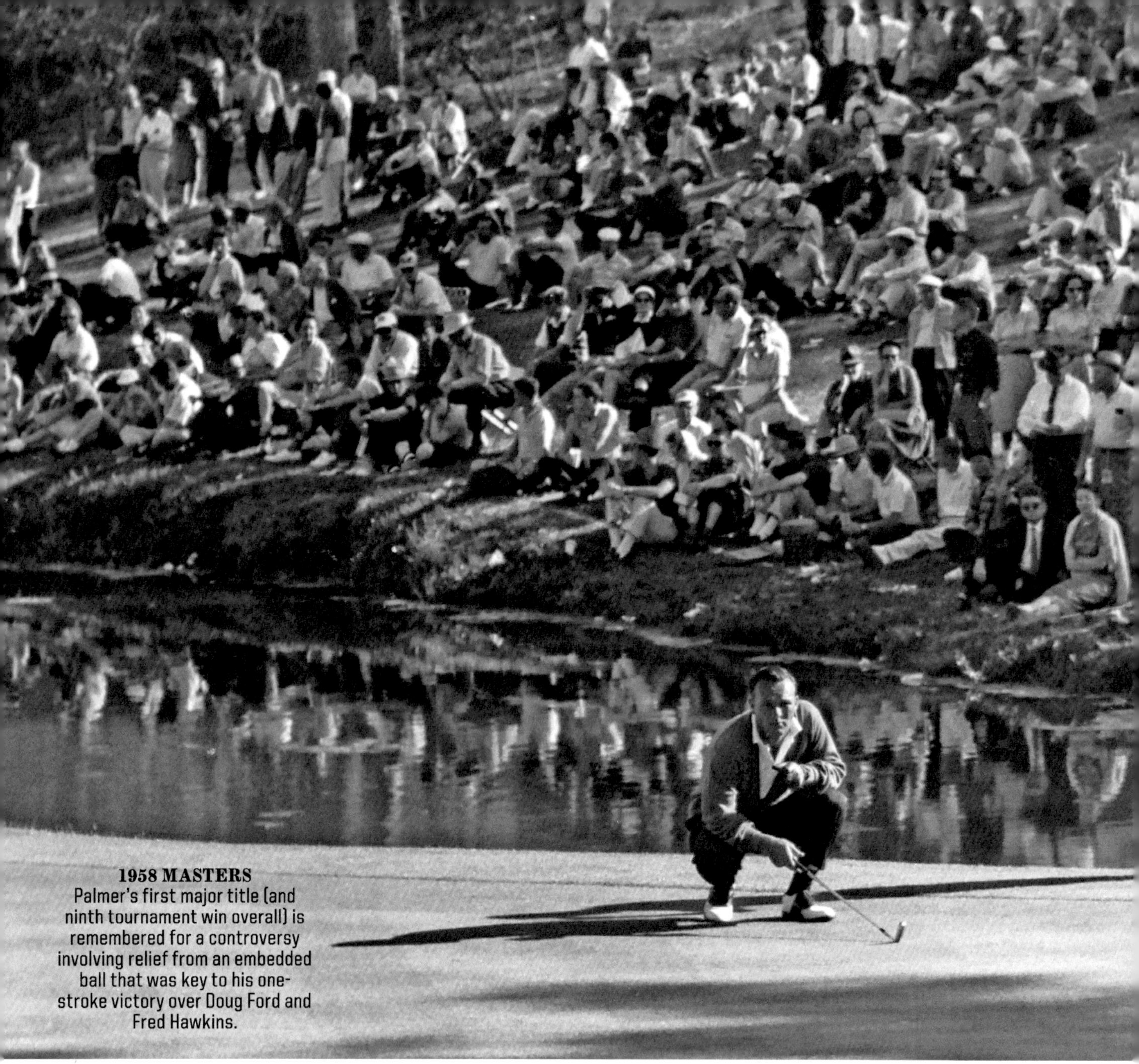

1958 MASTERS
Palmer's first major title (and ninth tournament win overall) is remembered for a controversy involving relief from an embedded ball that was key to his one-stroke victory over Doug Ford and Fred Hawkins.

THE MAJORS

Seven Big Ones

On golf's most exalted stages, Palmer demonstrated a flair for drama as well as for victory

AUGUSTA NATIONAL/GETTY IMAGES

1960 U.S. OPEN
This was Palmer at his most electric. He began the final round seven strokes back but raced up the leaderboard with a stunning six birdies in the first seven holes. After this and his Masters win two months prior, Herbert Warren Wind wrote in SI, "What can you say about Arnold Palmer? Nothing seems beyond his doing."

JOHN G. ZIMMERMAN

1960 MASTERS
With a 27-foot putt on the 17th hole and a six-iron at the flag on 18, Palmer finished birdie-birdie to top Ken Venturi. After his putt at 18, "it took Arnold a moment to realize it was all over, all won," wrote Herbert Warren Wind. "He retrieved his ball and walked a normal stride when he suddenly started jumping all over the place."

1961 BRITISH OPEN
Palmer played his first British Open in 1960, finishing second, and on his return trip he scored a one-stroke victory over Great Britain's Dai Rees at Royal Birkdale. Palmer was the only American in the top 10, but his success helped attract more U.S. players to the Open.

TALKING SPORT/PHOTOSHOT/UPPA/ZUMA

1962 BRITISH OPEN
Palmer attacked Royal Troon, and by week's end he brought the course to its knees and lifted the claret jug. He finished six strokes ahead of Australia's Kel Nagle and thirteen strokes ahead of third-place finishers Phil Rodgers and Brian Huggett.

BOB THOMAS/GETTY IMAGES

1962 MASTERS
This win required two comebacks. Palmer needed birdies on the 16th (with a 45-foot putt) and 17th to scramble into a tie for the lead on Sunday. Then in Monday's full-round playoff he trailed by three after nine holes, but surged on the back stretch to win by three strokes, topping Gary Player (left) and Dow Finsterwald.

AUGUSTA NATIONAL/GETTY IMAGES

JAMES DRAKE

1964 MASTERS
Palmer, presenting his scorecard, won by six strokes with a performance that was both dominant and controlled. "This week I decided not to be careless," he said.

THE U.S. OPEN

There's Never Been An Open Like It

The past, future and present came together on one incredible day at Cherry Hills in 1960 as Palmer caught Hogan and Nicklaus

BY DAN JENKINS

THEY WERE the most astonishing four hours in golf since Mary, Queen of Scots, found out what dormie meant and invented the back nine. And they still seem as significant to the game as, for instance, the day Arnold Palmer began hitching up his trousers, or the moment Jack Nicklaus decided to thin down and let his hair fluff, or that interlude in the pro shop when Ben Hogan selected his first white cap.

Small wonder that no sportswriter was capable of outlining it against a bright blue summer sky and letting the four adjectives ride again: It was too big, too wildly exciting, too crazily suspenseful, too suffocatingly dramatic. What exactly happened? Oh, not much, just a routine collision of three decades at one historical intersection.

On that afternoon, in the span of just 18 holes, we witnessed the arrival of Nicklaus, the coronation of Palmer and the end of Hogan. Nicklaus was a 20-year-old amateur who would own the 1970s. Palmer was a 30-year-old pro who would dominate the 1960s. Hogan was a 47-year-old immortal who had overwhelmed the 1950s.

While they had a fine supporting cast, it was primarily these three men who waged war for the U.S. Open title on that Saturday of June 18, 1960. The battle was continuous, under a steaming Colorado sun at Cherry Hills Country Club in Englewood. Things happened to the three of them and around them—all over the place—from about 1:45 until the shadows began to lengthen over the elms and cottonwoods, the wandering creek and yawning lake of Cherry Hills, host to our grandest championship.

In those days there was something in sport known as Open Saturday. It is no longer a part of golf, thanks to television—no thanks, actually. But it was a day like no other: a day on which the best golfers in the world were required to play 36 holes because it had always seemed to the USGA that a prolonged test of physical and mental stamina should go into the earning of the game's most important title. Thus, Open Saturday lent itself to wondrous comebacks and horrendous collapses, and it provided a full day's ration of every emotion familiar to the athlete competing under pressure for a prize so important as to be beyond the comprehension of most people.

Open Saturday had been an institution with the USGA since its fourth annual championship, in 1898. There had been thrillers before 1960. Saturdays that had tested the Bobby Joneses, Walter Hagens, Gene Sarazens, Harry Vardons, Francis Ouimets, Byron Nelsons, Sam Sneads—and, of course, the Ben Hogans—not to forget the occasional unknowns like John L. Black, Roland Hancock and Lee Mackey, all of them performing in wonderfully predictable and unexpectedly horrible ways, and so writing the history of the game in that one event, the National Open.

But any serious scholar of the sport, or anyone fortunate enough to have been there at Cherry Hills, is aware that the Open Saturday of Arnold, Ben and Jack was something very special—a U.S. Open that in meaning for the game continues to dwarf all of the others.

JOHN G. ZIMMERMAN

FROM SPORTS ILLUSTRATED
JUNE 19, 1978

ROCKY MOUNTAIN HIGH
After his victory Palmer joyfully launched his visor as he celebrated an unprecedented comeback on the 18th green in Englewood, Colo.

BETTMANN/GETTY IMAGES

The casual fan will remember 1960 as the year that old Arnie won when he shot a 65 in the last round and became the real Arnold Palmer. Threw his visor in the air, smoked a bunch of cigarettes, chipped in, drove a ball through a tree trunk, tucked in his shirttail and lived happily ever after with Winnie and President Eisenhower.

And that is pretty much what happened. But there is a constant truth about tournament golf: Other men have to lose a championship before one man can win it. And never has the final 18 of an Open produced as many losers as Cherry Hills did in 1960. When it was over, there were as many stretcher cases as there were shouts of "Whoo-ha, go get 'em, Arnie!" And that stood to reason after you considered that in those insane four hours Palmer came from seven strokes off the lead and from 15th place to grab a championship he had never even been in contention for.

Naturally, Palmer had arrived in Denver as the favorite. Two months earlier he had taken his second Masters with what was beginning to be known to the wire services as a "charge." He had almost been confirmed as The Player of the New Era, though not quite. But as late as noon on Open Saturday, after three rounds of competition, you would hardly have heard his name mentioned in Denver. A list of the leaders through 54 holes shows how hopeless his position seemed.

The scoreboard read:

MIKE SOUCHAK . . . . 68 . . .67 . . . 73. . .208
JULIUS BOROS . . . . 73 . . 69 . . .68. . . 210
DOW FINSTERWALD . . . . . . 71 . . 69 . . .70. . . 210
JERRY BARBER . . . . 69 . . .71 . . .70. . . 210
BEN HOGAN . . . . 75 . . .67 . . .69. . . 211
JACK NICKLAUS . . . . 71 . . .71 . . .69. . . 211
JACK FLECK . . . . 70 . . .70 . . .72. . . 212
JOHNNY POTT . . . . 75 . . 68 . . .69. . . 212
DON CHERRY . . . . 70 . . .71 . . . 71. . . 212
GARY PLAYER . . . . 70 . . .72 . . . 71. . . 213
SAM SNEAD . . . . 72 . . 69 . . .73. . . 214
BILLY CASPER . . . . 71 . . .70 . . .73. . . 214
DUTCH HARRISON . . . . 74 . . .70 . . .70. . . 214
BOB SHAVE . . . . 72 . . .71 . . . 71. . . 214
ARNOLD PALMER . . . . 72 . . .71 . . .72. . . 215

Right up until the last hole of the first 18 on Saturday, this Open had belonged exclusively to Mike Souchak, a long-hitting, highly popular pro who seldom allowed his career to get in the way of a social engagement. His blazing total of 135 after 36 holes was an Open record. And as he stood on the 18th tee of Saturday's morning round, he needed only a par-4 for a 71 and a four-stroke lead.

Then came an incident that gave everyone a foreboding about the afternoon. On Souchak's backswing, a camera clicked loudly. Souchak's drive soared out of bounds, and he took a double bogey 6 for a 73. He never really recovered from the jolt. While the lead would remain his well into the afternoon—long after Arnold had begun his sprint—you could see Souchak painfully allowing the tournament to slip away from him. He was headed for the slow death of a finishing 75 and another near miss, like the one he had experienced the previous year in the Open at Winged Foot.

Much has been written about Arnold Palmer in the locker room at Cherry Hills between rounds on Open Saturday.

JOHN G. ZIMMERMAN

TURNS OF FORTUNE
Hogan's chances disappeared when he hit his ball into the water on the 17th hole (opposite), while Palmer kept rolling, playing the back nine at one under par.

WHAT DID YOU SAY? Before Palmer's round a reporter told him he was too far back to win, but afterward Arnie was posing by the press tent scoreboard.

AP

It has become a part of golfing lore. As it happened, I was there, one of four people with Arnold. Two of the others were golfers—Ken Venturi and Bob Rosburg, who were even further out of the tournament than Palmer—and the fourth was Bob Drum, a writer then with the *Pittsburgh Press.* It was a position that allowed Drum to enjoy the same close relationship with Palmer that *The Atlanta Journal*'s O.B. Keeler once had with Bobby Jones.

It was too hot to believe that you could actually see snowcaps on the Rockies on the skyline. As Palmer, Venturi and Rosburg sat in the locker room, there was no talk at all of who might win, only of how short and inviting the course was playing, of how Souchak, with the start he had, would probably shoot 269 if the tournament were a Pensacola Classic instead of the Open. Arnold was cursing the first hole at Cherry Hills, a 346-yard par-4 with an elevated tee. Three times he had just missed driving the green. As he left to join Paul Harney for their 1:42 starting time on the final 18, the thing on his mind was trying to drive that green. It would be his one Cherry Hills accomplishment.

"If I drive the green and get a birdie or an eagle, I might shoot 65," Palmer said. "What'll that do?"

Drum said, "Nothing. You're too far back."

"It would give me 280," Palmer said. "Doesn't 280 always win the Open?"

"Yeah, when Hogan shoots it," Drum said, laughing heartily at his own wit. Drum was a large Irishman with a P.A. system for a voice and a gag writer's knowledge of diplomacy.

Arnold lingered at the doorway, looking at us as if he were waiting for a better exit line. "Go on, boy," Drum said. "Get out of here. Go make your seven or eight birdies and shoot 73. I'll see you later."

Drum had been writing Palmer stories since Palmer was the West Pennsylvania amateur champion. On a Fort Worth paper I had been writing Hogan stories for 10 years, but I had also become a friend of Palmer's because I was a friend of Drum's. Palmer left the room, but we didn't, for the simple reason that the leader, Souchak, would not start his last round for another 15 or 20 minutes. But the fun began before that, when word drifted back that Palmer had indeed driven the first green and two-putted for a birdie. He had not carried the ball 346 yards in the air, but he had nailed it good enough for it to burn a path through the high weeds the USGA had nurtured in front of the green to prevent just such a thing from happening. Palmer had in fact barely missed his eagle putt from 20 feet.

Frankly, we thought nothing of it. Nor did we think much of the news that Arnold had chipped in from 35 feet for a birdie at the second. What did get Drum's attention was the distant thunder, which signaled that Arnold had birdied the 3rd hole. We were standing near the putting green by the clubhouse, and we had just decided to meander out toward Souchak when Drum said, "Care to join me at the 4th hole?"

I said, "He's still not in the golf tournament."

"He will be," Drum said.

And rather instinctively we broke into a downhill canter.

As we arrived at the green, Palmer was drilling an 18-foot birdie putt into the cup. He was now four under through 4, two under for the championship, only three strokes behind Souchak, and there were a lot of holes left to play.

We stooped under the ropes at the 5th tee and awaited Arnold's entrance. He came in hitching up the pants and gazed down the fairway. Spotting us, he strolled over.

"Fancy seeing you here," he said with a touch of slyness.

Then he drank the rest of my Coke, smoked one of my cigarettes and failed to birdie the hole, a par-5. On the other hand he more than made up for it by sinking a curving 25-footer for a birdie at the par-3 6th. At the 7th he hit another splendid wedge to within six feet of the flag. He made the putt. And the cheers that followed told everybody on the golf course that Arnold Palmer had birdied six of the first seven holes.

It was history-book stuff. And yet for all of those heroics it was absolutely unreal to look up at a scoreboard out on the course and learn that Arnold Palmer still wasn't leading the Open. Some kid named Jack Nicklaus was. That beefy guy from Columbus paired with Hogan, playing two groups ahead of Palmer. The amateur.

"My man's knocked 'em all out," said Drum. "They just haven't felt the shock waves yet."

Out in 32. Five under now for the tournament.

Drum sized up the scoreboard for everyone around him.

"The fat kid's five under, and the whole world's four under," he said.

That was true one minute and not true the next. By the whole world Drum meant Palmer, Hogan, Souchak, Boros, Fleck, Finsterwald, Barber, Cherry, etc. It was roughly 3:30 then, and for the next half hour it was impossible to know who was leading, coming on, falling back or what. Palmer further complicated things by taking a bogey at the 8th. He parred the 9th and was out in a stinging 30, five under on the round. But in harsh truth, as I suggested to Drum at the time, he was still only three under for the tournament and two strokes off the pace of Nicklaus or Boros or Souchak—possibly all three. And God knows, I said, what Hogan, Fleck and Cherry were doing while we were there talking.

Fleck had put almost the same kind of torch to Cherry Hills' front nine holes that Palmer had. Fleck had birdied five of the first six, with a bogey included. He would wind up in what would look like a 200-way tie for third place at 283. Don Cherry, the other amateur in contention, was the last man with a chance. There was a moment in the press tent when everyone was talking about Palmer's victory, and somebody calculated that Cherry could shoot 33 on the back nine and win. Cherry was due to finish shortly after dark. He quickly made a couple of bogeys, however, and that was that. But meanwhile we were out on the course thinking about Palmer's chances in all of this when Drum made his big pronouncement of the day.

"My man's knocked 'em all out," he said. "They just haven't felt the shock waves yet."

History has settled for Drum's analysis, and perhaps that is the truth of the matter after all. The story of the 1960 Open has been compressed into one sentence: Arnold Palmer birdied six of the first seven holes and won.

But condensations kill. What is missing is everything that happened after four o'clock. The part about Souchak losing the lead for the first time only after he bogeyed the 9th hole. The part about Nicklaus blowing the lead he held all by himself when he took three ghastly putts from only 10 feet at the 13th. This was the first real indication that they were all coming back to Palmer now, for Nicklaus's bogey dropped him into a four-way tie with Palmer, Boros and Fleck.

But so much more is still missing. Nicklaus's inexperience as a young amateur cost him another three-putt bogey at the 14th hole, and so, as suddenly as he had grabbed the lead, he was out of it. Then it was around 4:45, and Palmer was sharing the lead with Hogan and Fleck, at four under. But like Nicklaus, Fleck would leave it on the greens. Boros had started leaving it on the greens and in the bunkers somewhat earlier. He was trapped at the 14th and the 18th, and in between he blew a three-footer. In the midst of all this Palmer was playing a steady back side of one birdie and eight pars on the way to his 65. And until the last two holes of the championship, the only man who had performed more steadily than Palmer, or seemed to be enduring the Open stress with as much steel as he, was—no surprise—Ben Hogan.

It was close to 5:30 when Hogan and Palmer were alone at four under in the championship, and the two of them, along with everybody else—literally everyone on the golf course—had wound up on the 17th hole, the 71st of the tournament.

The 17th at Cherry Hills is a long, straightaway par-5, 548 yards, with a green fronted by an evil pond. In 1960 it was a drive, a layup and a pitch. And there they all were. Hogan and Nicklaus contemplating their pitch shots as the twosome of Boros and Player waited to hit their second shots, while the twosome of Palmer and Paul Harney stood back on the tee.

Hogan was faced with a delicate shot of about 50 yards to a pin that was sitting altogether too close to the water for him to try anything risky. He had hit 34 straight greens in regulation that Saturday. He needed only a par-par finish for a 69, which would have been his third consecutive subpar round in the tournament. He had to think this might be his last real chance to capture another Open. And nobody understood better than Hogan what it meant to reach the clubhouse first with a good score in a major championship.

Armed with this expertise as I knelt in the rough and watched Hogan address the shot, I brilliantly whispered to Drum:

AP

TO BE CONTINUED
Palmer (left) won the day, but Nicklaus, then a 20-year-old amateur, showed the skills that would soon have him collecting major titles.

"He probably thinks he needs another birdie with Arnold behind him, but I'll guarantee you, Ben'll be over the water." At which point Hogan hit the ball in the water.

He made a bogey 6. And in trying to erase that blunder on the 18th with a huge drive, which might produce a birdie, he hooked his tee shot into the lake and suffered a triple-bogey 7. Only 30 minutes after he had been a co-leader with just two holes to go, Hogan finished in a tie for ninth place, four strokes away.

Second place then was left to the 20-year-old with the crew cut. All in all, these were tremendous performances by an aging Hogan and a young Nicklaus. The two of them had come the closest to surviving Palmer's shock waves.

It was later on, back in the locker room, long after Palmer had slung his visor in the air for the photographers, that Ben Hogan said the truest thing of all about the day. Ben would know best. He said, "I guess they'll say I lost it. Well, one more foot, and the wedge on 17 would have been perfect. But I'll tell you something. I played 36 holes today with a kid who should have won this Open by 10 shots."

Jack Nicklaus would start winning major titles soon enough as a pro, of course. But wasn't it nice to have Arnold around first?

Arnie & Jack

Golf's epic rivalry began with a charged meeting on a humble track in Ohio

BY IAN O'CONNOR

MAN TO MAN
By then both stars, the friends did some table talking at the 1965 PGA Championship in Ligonier, Pa.

WALTER IOOSS JR.

THE ELDERS at Athens Country Club in Ohio had cobbled together a big day to honor one of their own, Dow Finsterwald, and needed to fill the last slot on their VIP list. They wanted a man and settled for a boy. Fred Swearingen, club president, had been struck by a sudden thought. He would call up this hotshot kid in Columbus and ask him if he would care to play 18 holes with Finsterwald, fresh off his victory in the PGA Championship, and Dow's good friend Arnold Palmer, that year's winner of the Masters.

Swearingen found a listing for Charlie Nicklaus's drugstore.

"Is your boy interested in playing with the PGA champ and the Masters champ?" Swearingen asked.

"I'm sure he is," Charlie said. "He's right here. I'll put him on."

Without blinking, Jack Nicklaus told Swearingen that he'd be happy to bring his game to the southeast corner of Ohio. "I'll get my dad to take me," Jack said.

He was 18 years old in September 1958, and his father would drive him to his first face-to-face encounter with Palmer, who was only days removed from his 29th birthday and just months removed from his first victory at Augusta National, the one that hinted at the dawn of a new era in professional golf.

This wouldn't be the first time young Nicklaus had seen Palmer in the flesh. At the 1954 Ohio Amateur, outside Toledo, Jackie was a 14-year-old qualifier who stumbled upon a dark, solitary figure on the Sylvania Country Club driving range, raging at ball after ball in a Biblical rain.

Nicklaus didn't know the man's identity but was mesmerized. Under cover, from about 40 yards away, Nicklaus stared at the stranger in the rain suit for 10 minutes.

Palmer was from Latrobe, in western Pennsylvania, but he was eligible for the Ohio Amateur because of his time in Cleveland, where he was a member of the U.S. Coast Guard and, of all things, a frustrated paint salesman. He was pounding nine-irons, making them turn right to left, commanding them with a musculature that belonged to a middleweight fighter. Nicklaus saw a relentless series of angry line drives that never rose more than six feet off the ground.

This was two days before the start of the state amateur, and Nicklaus was the only other competitor on the course. The storms wouldn't let up. Jackie was soaked, but he couldn't tear himself away from a scene that could have been cut right out of a Tiger Woods credit-card ad nearly half a century later. There are no rainy days.

Palmer didn't even know young Nicklaus was there. Arnold was unwittingly giving the heir to his future throne a lesson in hard-earned royalty. Nicklaus loved the raw commitment, the brute strength. He had never seen anyone attack a golf ball quite like that.

Finally, Jackie stepped inside the clubhouse. "Who is that guy out on the driving range?" he asked. "Man, is he strong."

A voice identified Palmer, the defending state champ.

Palmer would make it two in a row long after Nicklaus lost to someone named Dale Bittner on the 19th hole. Bittner would be a fleeting thought, gone just like that. Nicklaus went home to tell friends and neighbors all about the golfer swinging in the rain, the carnival strongman who crushed opponents with his frighteningly large hands.

Four years later, when Charlie Nicklaus made the 75-mile drive with his growing boy for the date with Palmer, Jack had left his awe at home, left it there in a closet cluttered with everything else he'd outgrown.

"The guy had basically just started winning majors," Nicklaus says. "Did I know Arnold Palmer was a good player? You're darn right. But was I ever in awe of what he did? Probably not."

No, the teenage Nicklaus wasn't short on confidence. Having recently entered his sophomore year at Ohio State, he had built himself a remarkable record on the junior circuit. He had won the Ohio State Open as a 16-year-old competing against pros. He'd already played in two U.S. Opens, making the cut earlier that year at Southern Hills. He'd won a national Jaycees championship, and he had contended in his first Tour event, standing a shot off the lead after two rounds of the 1958 Rubber City Open before finishing 12th.

Jack wasn't about to make a fuss over Palmer, who had only one major championship to his name to go with the 1954 U.S. Amateur title. Nicklaus would let the people of Athens do the fussin' for him.

PALMER WAS quite a catch for a community in the Appalachian foothills, a college town of 15,000, about half of them students at Ohio University. To the coal miners and farmers of the depressed pockets surrounding the sanctuary of higher education, Palmer's arrival, according to George Strode, sports editor of *The Athens Messenger*, "was like the second coming of Christ."

The son of an Athens lawyer, Finsterwald was the one who had booked the main attraction. His friendship with Palmer was born of the matches they played as college rivals, Dow as a star at Ohio, Arnold at Wake Forest.

Palmer had shot a 29 on the first nine they played together. In one Ohio-Wake match, with Arnold and Dow tied at the turn, Palmer declared, "I'll bet you a tub of beer I shoot 32 or better on the back."

Palmer shot 31. The pecking order in their relationship established forevermore, Palmer and Finsterwald became what one pro described as "ass---- buddies."

Dow told everyone to count Arnold in. "Give him a call," Swearingen said.

"Hell, give him a call yourself," Finsterwald responded. "Here's his number. He's there right now."

Sure enough, Arnold was home in Latrobe and eager to participate in a day to honor Athens's favorite son. Swearingen told Palmer that he would send him a plane ticket to Columbus and drive him to town.

"You've got an airport in Athens, don't you?" Palmer asked.

Jack left his awe at home, left it there in a closet cluttered with everything else he'd outgrown.

"Well, we've got a landing strip at the university," Swearingen said.

"I don't need a ticket then. I'll fly right in."

If Palmer hadn't chosen golf as his vocation, he most likely would have become a commercial pilot. At first he was scared to death to fly. Once, when he was an amateur golfer en route to Chattanooga on a DC-3, he was startled by a ball of fire rolling up and down the aisle. "I immediately found out that it was static electricity," Palmer says, "and that's when I decided I would learn to fly and understand what was happening."

He overcame his fear out of necessity—he wanted to spend as much time with his family as possible and driving from Tour stop to Tour stop was no way to accomplish that.

So he earned his pilot's license. Palmer flew into Athens with his wife, Winnie. Swearingen picked them up and drove the Palmers to the home of Finsterwald's cousin Jean Sprague, where they would spend the night and then rise early on the morning of Thursday, Sept. 25, 1958, when Arnold would pay tribute to his good friend and play golf with Jack Nicklaus for the first time.

Swearingen would plan the day around a parade and a match involving two two-man teams. The fourth competitor was an amateur, Howard Baker Saunders, a six-time Southeastern Ohio Golf Association champ out of nearby Gallipolis and a top player on the Ohio State team 15 years before Nicklaus would fill the same role. Saunders would have turned pro if he hadn't suffered from osteomyelitis, an infection of the bone that left him with a bad limp. With one leg shorter than the other, Saunders wore one shoe with a five-inch heel to level his playing field.

Court Street was packed for the morning parade. Finsterwald, Palmer, Nicklaus and Saunders rode in their own convertibles, tops down, waving like returning war heroes at a delirious crowd of 1,200. The mayor presented Finsterwald with a key to the city. Speeches were given, autographs were signed, pictures were taken. Michael DiSalle, busy running a successful campaign for the governorship of Ohio, joked that he had picked the wrong day to come to Athens.

No politician could match the golfers' star power. And nobody cared that more people had come to see Arnold than to see Dow.

When the hourlong ceremony was complete, Swearingen had the golfers go fishing before it was time to head to the club. He grabbed some rods out of his store, gave them to Finsterwald, Palmer and Nicklaus, and steered them to a pond full of catfish.

Finsterwald and Palmer knew their way around the hills

HEY, IT'S YOU AGAIN!
From 1962 to '65 Palmer and Nicklaus took turns winning the Masters and donning the green jacket at Augusta.

JAMES DRAKE

THE COUNTRY CLUB

Palmer, who won 22 Ryder Cup matches—a record for an American—paired with Nicklaus during a U.S. victory in St. Louis in 1971.

RICH CLARKSON

and streams of Appalachia, "but Jack was a city boy," Swearingen says. Jack cast his line over the hillside and got it caught in some rocks. He refused to go down and loosen it—he was afraid a snake might be waiting for him. "No, Jack wasn't roaming any hills in Columbus," Swearingen continues. "The only hills he ever roamed were at Scioto Country Club or in that real nice suburb of his, Upper Arlington."

Over time Nicklaus would grow sensitive to any talk that he was a rich daddy's boy, especially when the talk was inspired by Palmer's past. Arnold was the son of a greenkeeper, the sod-stained child on the other side of the country-club grass. People adored his Horatio Alger tale and assumed that Nicklaus had never spent a day of his youth with any tool in his hands that didn't come out of a shiny new golf bag.

But as an 18-year-old prodigy driven by ambition, Nicklaus carried something of a pauper's chip on his shoulder. Remarkably enough, the kid refused to treat his first meeting with Palmer as a brush with uncommon skill and fame. He merely saw the reigning king of Augusta National as another hurdle to clear, another guy to beat. "I don't think he was so excited to play [Palmer]," Swearingen says.

NESTLED ATOP a hill five miles from the parade route, Athens Country Club was a playground for university professors and administrators and for the doctors, dentists and businessmen who had them as patients and clients. Theirs was a simple nine-hole, Donald Ross course, with alternate tees for the second nine. Put together, the nines measured 6,382 yards and played to a par 72. With a single dirt road (barely wide enough for two cars passing in opposite directions) leading into the club, Athens hardly looked like the center of the golf universe. But with the Tour season largely complete, this was the biggest game on the schedule. The sky was clear, and the temperature was in the upper 60s. A gallery of about 1,500 poured onto the grounds. Fans parked cars along the 7th fairway. In fact, fans parked in the yards of everyone who lived just off the course.

The sides were chosen, and Palmer, considered the strongest player, was paired with Nicklaus, considered the weakest because of his age. The four participants were warming up when the forces of fate intervened.

Nicklaus and Palmer would go head-to-head after all.

As Palmer and Finsterwald were swatting practice drives from the elevated tee on the 321-yard 1st hole, Nicklaus and Saunders were sent to the nearby 9th green to hit balls back toward the 9th tee. Jack swung with all his teenage might and immediately caused a stir.

A witness approached Kermit Blosser, the Ohio U golf coach and de facto master of ceremonies. "Hey," the man told Blosser, "you ought to get that Nicklaus kid to hit against Arnold on number 1. He's really moving it down there."

Blosser summoned Nicklaus to the 1st tee, where Palmer was flexing his comic-book biceps. The golf coach had a microphone, and he was about to become a play-by-play man. A short, precise driver known for his cautious, anti-Arnold game, Finsterwald stepped aside as Palmer accepted the challenge.

Palmer carried himself with John Wayne swagger. Nicklaus looked like an extra on his movie set.

The fairways were dry and fast, allowing the mad bombers to add an extra 15 or 20 yards to their prodigious drives. Palmer and Nicklaus took a few warmup swings. Jack's technically sound form appeared torn from the pages of a manual, with one exception: His right elbow flew away from his side. Palmer couldn't help but notice the flaw, but he wasn't in any position to mock another player's mechanics. His swing was punctuated by the least aesthetically pleasing follow-through in golf. In the immediate wake of impact Palmer abruptly jerked the club above his head and appeared to begin wrestling with a rattlesnake, a gushing water hose, or both.

Nicklaus, meanwhile, had a full follow-through and none of Palmer's gyrations. Their games were as different as their backgrounds and body types. Nicklaus came from German stock, Palmer from Scotch, Irish and English. Nicklaus had thighs that looked like redwood trunks; Palmer had hands that could crush a watermelon.

Palmer carried himself with a John Wayne swagger and an Errol Flynn flair. He didn't walk to his tee shots; he marched. After surveying his target and flicking his cigarette to the grass, Palmer approached his ball as if he were a cowboy loading up at the O.K. Corral.

Nicklaus? He looked like an extra on Palmer's movie set. "A little plump kid with real short hair," Swearingen says. The blond Nicklaus walked around with a god-awful buzz cut, and his pale skin could blotch up in the summertime; it would never accommodate an even tan like Palmer's.

Arnold and Jack both stood about 5' 10", so they looked each other squarely in the eye when they shook hands on a tee box for the first time. For all of Palmer's smoky, leading-man looks, Nicklaus might have had an advantage here: Even as a kid his piercing blue eyes had already cut through many a foe on the 1st tee.

BLOSSER HAD arranged for four of his Ohio players to serve as caddies, and he had Dow Reichley, Bill Santor, Larry Snyder and Charlie Vandlik make their way down to the 1st green to shag the driving-contest balls. "I know they had a bet," Reichley says of Palmer and Nicklaus. "I don't know how much it was for."

Something more important than a few bucks was on the line here. Palmer was a pro, Nicklaus an amateur. Palmer was a man, Nicklaus a boy.

Hundreds of fans closed in around the 1st tee, giving it the feel of a boxing ring. The golfers and fans looked out from their

A KING AND A BEAR WALK INTO A BAR
The titans of golf and business enjoy a laugh at the 1974 World Open Golf Tournament at Pinehurst.

HEINZ KLUETMEIER

elevated perch at a hole that turned slightly left to right. On the right side of the fairway, rows of pines stretched toward the green. Two bunkers were lurking to the left of the putting surface, one about 30 yards short of the fringe.

The 3rd green sat 35 downhill yards behind the 1st green. Nobody in his right mind believed that either competitor could drive his ball there—not in the age of persimmon clubs and balata balls.

Nicklaus took the honors, and his first drive was a monster. "He hit it so high," Santor says, "you could barely see it up in the sky."

The ball cleared the 1st green and stopped rolling only after it had traveled 356 yards. Santor picked up Nicklaus's ball on the 3rd green.

The caddie knew a thing or two about Jack's tape-measure power. As a high school senior in 1955 Santor had played in the same field with Nicklaus, an underclassman, in the state Jaycees tournament. Santor placed second. Nicklaus beat him by only 12 strokes.

Palmer had no such intimate knowledge of Nicklaus and his game. He had heard a few vague tales of the boy wonder from the Columbus area sweeping through the amateur ranks, but Palmer had enough to worry about with his own generation to lose any sleep over the next one.

Only, in Athens the future was suddenly now. Palmer teed up his ball, knowing he had almost no chance of matching the kid's first drive. He lashed at it with vile intentions, hoping to power his ball down to the 3rd green, but it stayed low, like most Palmer drives. Much lower than Nicklaus's ball. "Arnold hit a big hook," Swearingen says. "It hit short of the 1st green and bounced downhill to the left."

Nicklaus then ripped his second drive. As Santor stood near the 1st green, he squinted to track the ball's high, majestic flight. Again, Nicklaus put his drive on the 3rd green, more than 350 yards away.

Again, Palmer failed to match it, unleashing another low, screaming hook.

"Jack was outhitting Arnold by 35, 40 yards," Santor says. "I could hear the crowd yelling around the 1st tee."

His face three shades of red, Palmer shot an incredulous look at Nicklaus. "My God," he said, "no man hits it that far. It's men like you who make problems for us."

Blosser was dumbfounded. He had never seen a player of any age put a drive from the 1st tee onto the 3rd green, never mind two drives. The de facto master of ceremonies decided to make a show of it.

"Mr. Palmer," Blosser barked loudly enough for everyone to hear, "can you tell me why you're hooking that ball so violently?"

"Because I'm trying to hit it too damn hard just to keep up with this kid," Palmer responded, flustered.

It was a lost cause. Palmer would later claim that he had won this long-ball contest, but witnesses reported that the players hit about 15 drives each, and with the aid of some friendly bounces Arnold kept up with Jack maybe three or four times.

Palmer was embarrassed and a little upset that Blosser called extra attention to it. But Palmer still had the better-ball match coming up, and even though Nicklaus would be his teammate, he could still outplay him, still show the boy what was what.

Blosser's players drew straws to see who would caddie for whom. Snyder got Palmer, Vandlik got Nicklaus, Santor got Finsterwald, and Reichley got Saunders.

Finsterwald and Saunders were the favorites, as most assumed that young Nicklaus would be a drag on Palmer. All but emasculated by Nicklaus in the game before the game, Palmer opened the team match with a fury, hitting his first approach shot to within a foot of the hole, tapping in for the easy 3 while the others made par. Palmer added birdies on two of the next three holes. If Palmer couldn't beat Nicklaus in the driving contest, he would make darn sure that everyone saw him carry Nicklaus during this match.

Palmer nearly aced the par-3 8th with a four-iron after Snyder, his caddie, advised him to clear the pond with a five-iron. Another birdie.

Palmer settled for a six-under 30 on the front side. His teammate, Nicklaus, made the turn at 35. Saunders kept his team in the match with a 33, while Finsterwald struggled to a 36. At the break Palmer-Nicklaus held a 3-up lead.

Not that the team competition was the be-all and end-all. The crowd was buzzing over the possibility that Palmer could shoot 59 or that he could at least break Finsterwald's course record. Among the caddies Nicklaus was also a prime subject of conversation.

Like Santor, Snyder had seen Jack up close in tournament play. In 1952, a 14-year-old Snyder went up against a 12-year-old Nicklaus in the district juniors, and the older player prevailed in 19 holes. "And I bet he outweighed me by 40 pounds," Snyder recalls. "By the time Jack was 18 his power was phenomenal."

That power moved the earth in Athens, and the Ohio U players serving as caddies couldn't fathom the noise made when Nicklaus's clubface made contact with the ball. "The crack, the boom," Reichley says. "It was a supersonic sound."

Nicklaus drove the green on the 330-yard 10th hole, landing his tee shot pin high and six feet from the cup. He missed the eagle putt and settled for a 3. Palmer also birdied the hole, turning the gallery on its ear. "Watching Jack and Arnie," Reichley says, "we were awestruck."

Finsterwald went on a birdie binge to make up for his lackluster front nine, but Saunders faded. Palmer and Nicklaus were in the clear. Both were outmuscling the course, though Palmer was making more putts.

The caddies were watching Palmer's every purposeful step. He was the leading money winner on the Tour at that point, yet he didn't walk with an air of superiority. "So down-to-earth," Snyder says. "He never said an unkind word to me, never frowned, never acted as if I should've known better to do this or that."

The Ohio U boys also watched the body language between Palmer and Nicklaus. No one could imagine then that these two figures—separated by more than 10 years—would someday make up the greatest rivalry the game has ever known.

After being emasculated in the game before the game, Palmer opened the team match with a fury.

But there was no extra effort on either player's part to bridge their generation gap. "Arnold and Jack were cordial," Reichley says, "but Nicklaus wasn't much of a talker. . . . He kind of stuck to the business of the day."

That business was drumming every player on the course. Nicklaus wasn't nearly as interested in winning the team competition as he was in shooting the lowest score. He didn't want to defeat Finsterwald and Saunders. He wanted to defeat Finsterwald, Saunders and Palmer.

Nicklaus would win only low amateur honors, his 68 beating Saunders's 71. Finsterwald saved face in his own backyard, edging Nicklaus by a shot. Palmer sank a 50-footer at the 16th and made an easy two-putt par on the 18th for a 62, celebrating Finsterwald's day by breaking his friend's Athens record by one.

Palmer said a few kind words about Nicklaus afterward but wasn't effusive in his praise. Over the decades, whenever asked about this day, Palmer would inevitably talk about Nicklaus's flying elbow, the one conspicuous flaw.

"I thought he was potentially good," Palmer says. "I noticed he had his right elbow, it was unattached. Let's say it swung out. . . . Until he got that elbow under control or kept that elbow closer, he might've had some problems with his game."

After the exhibition the golfers were off to a dinner held in Dow's honor. Palmer and Finsterwald helped themselves to a few cocktails while Charlie Nicklaus kept close watch over his boy. "I don't think either Arnold or I realized how great Jack was going to be," Finsterwald would say. "We didn't appreciate . . . the significance of what was taking place."

Finsterwald did make a speech at the dinner, and in it he predicted Nicklaus would have a "wonderful future" in golf. The other players spoke as well, and Nicklaus handled himself with surprising ease on the podium. Palmer told the audience he liked Jack's putting stroke. At the close of the evening, the man and the boy shared their final handshake and went their separate ways, Arnold back to the Tour, Jack back to Ohio State.

Swearingen would go on to become an NFL referee and make one of the most controversial calls in league history: the Immaculate Reception ruling that decided the 1972 Oakland Raiders–Pittsburgh Steelers playoff game. But first he officiated at golf's Immaculate Conception, the birth of a rivalry that would fuel the surging popularity of golf in the 1960s.

A driving contest in Appalachia. A meaningless exhibition on a middling nine-hole course. "That was the start of the whole Palmer and Nicklaus thing," Swearingen says. That was the start of a lifelong clash of titans that would play out in fairways and boardrooms across the globe.

THE HEAD AND THE HEART
Palmer once characterized his rivalry with Nicklaus as the contrast between instinctual and intellectual play.

WALTER IOOSS JR.

Beyond The Golf Course

Palmer's reach included books, clothes, design work—and one refreshing beverage

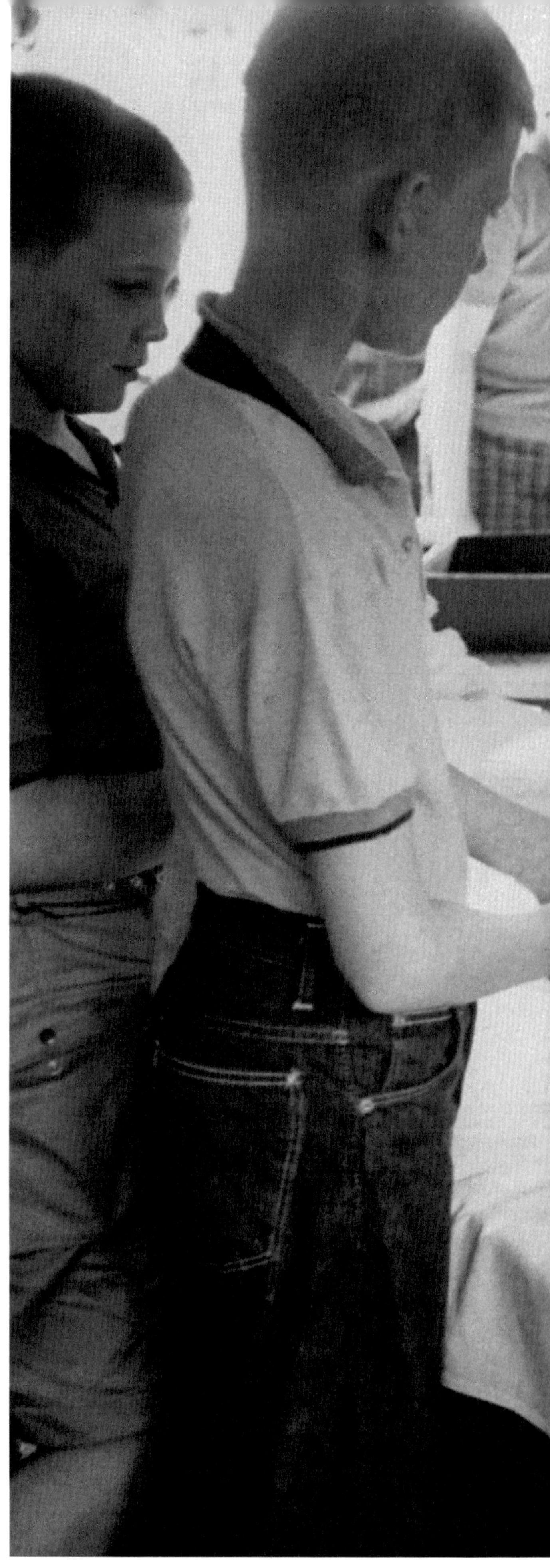

JOHN DOMINIS/THE LIFE PICTURE COLLECTION/GETTY IMAGES

BE LIKE ARNIE
Palmer, perhaps the game's greatest ambassador, had lines of clubs and balls, wrote 10 instructional books and offered children this golf-themed board game in 1962.

Arnold Palmer's
INSIDE GOLF
LEARN GOOD GOLF IN THE LIVING ROOM

Punch, June 30 1965

Orlon Orlon

Arnold Palmer plays in ORLON by Pringle

Pringle have designed these two new styles in ORLON* acrylic specially for Arnold Palmer, America's No 1 golfer. They are now available to all golfers and sportsmen through leading retailers and golf clubs. *Left:* Palmer sportshirt by Pringle in ORLON at 72/6. *Right:* Palmer Roll Collar Pullover by Pringle in ORLON at 65/-. Golfers who know prefer ORLON by Pringle.

ENDORSEMENTS
Orlon was but one of a multitude of products Palmer promoted; he also sold menswear for Sears, did TV ads for Hertz and drove a tractor for years in Pennzoil commercials.

POLITICS
In 1990, Palmer, whose popularity attracted elected officials, was invited to speak to Congress to honor his friend Dwight Eisenhower, the former president.

COURSE MASTER
Palmer, designer of many courses, owned Bay Hill (above) in Orlando, Fla., where he hosted a tournament won eight times by Tiger Woods.

CLOCKWISE FROM TOP LEFT: ADVERTISING ARCHIVE/THE EVERETT COLLECTION; RON EDMONDS/AP; SCOTT AUDETTE/AP; FRED VUICH

A LIQUID LEGEND

He poured lemonade into a pitcher of iced tea his wife had made. Then he ordered that hybrid concoction in a restaurant, a fan overheard, and a phenomenon spread by word of mouth. In 2001 Arizona Beverages began selling a half-and-half version. Arnie preferred more iced tea, but the general recipe is: Adjust the mix to your sweet/tart scale, sit back and sip.

LESLIE PARROTT/VAULT ARCHIVES/REDUX

LITTLE PRINCESS
Daughter Amy said that when her dad was at home "he was always all touchy and huggy. He's real emotional that way."

In His Castle

A 1960 photo session took a rare and intimate look at the king off the course

ROBERT HUNTZINGER

CLUBS SUIT HIM
Palmer relaxed at the Latrobe County Club (above) and ground golf clubs at home (opposite).

ROBERT HUNTZINGER (2)

"Arnold has had his share of good fortune in life, and the best fortune of all was marrying Winnie."

—FRIEND MARK H. MCCORMACK, SI, MARCH 6, 1967

ROBERT HUNTZINGER (3)

OFF-ROADING
Palmer enjoys a respite at home with Winnie and daughters Peggy and Amy, and also a chance to work his magic in the kitchen.

Sportsman Of the Year

In 1960 SPORTS ILLUSTRATED gave its signature award to a man who wowed fans with his game and his personality

BY RAY CAVE

ARNIE'S ASSAULT
Palmer won eight of the 27 tournaments he entered in 1960, and if he didn't come in first he was usually in the hunt, including a second-place finish at the British Open.

JERRY COOKE

SPORTING 1960 was international in scope. The XVII Olympics assured that. It reached an unparalleled audience. Television saw to that. And it infected the greatest number of people ever with a desire to take part themselves in sport. Growing incomes and a world at relative peace permitted that. And nowhere else did a 1960 sports personality command his field with quite the overwhelming ability and natural charm of Arnold Daniel Palmer.

Early in the year Palmer won three tour tournaments in a row, the first time that had been done since 1952. Then in April he came from behind to win the Masters by getting birdies on the last two holes in one of his typical final-day rushes to victory. In June he won the U.S. Open, starting the last 18 holes with a prodigious 346-yard drive to the first green at Colorado's Cherry Hills Country Club—perhaps the single most meaningful golf shot of the year, because he then went on to score six birdies on the first seven holes and record the strongest finish in that tournament's 60-year history. He teamed with Sam Snead to win the international Canada Cup for the U.S. in Ireland, and then lost the British Open at St. Andrews by a single stroke when another driving finish fell just short. ("I see a wee bit of Hogan in the laddie," said one discerning old Scot. "Aye, but he is a warm boy," answered his companion.)

By the end of the year Palmer had played in 27 tournaments, won eight of them, rarely finished worse than fifth. He had collected $80,738 in prize money, establishing a new record for golf earnings. Palmer made off with the prize money by combining the boldness of a Brinks bandit with the fearless confidence of a man on a flying trapeze, seeming to order the ball through sheer willpower to get into the hole.

His concentration as he addressed a golf shot was grimly intense, yet, unlike so many of his top competitors, he didn't retreat into an egocentric shell to maintain that concentration. It was Palmer who would sit around a clubhouse sipping a whisky and talking golf after a round, who was enough of a ham to delight in TV appearances, enough of a daredevil to fly a supersonic Navy jet and enough of a frustrated football player to throw the ball around with local high school kids. With his golf credo— "Hit it hard"—that horrifies traditionalists, his boyish enthusiasm, his athletic good looks and irrepressible will to win, he has dominated the game as no one has since the heyday of Ben Hogan.

Thus he has ended his sport's long wait for a fresh, vibrant personality, bringing a new age to golf: The Palmer Era. It is for this that the editors of SPORTS ILLUSTRATED select him as Sportsman of the Year.

FROM SPORTS ILLUSTRATED
JANUARY 9, 1961

The son of a golf professional, Arnold Palmer was born to the links as kings are born to the purple. He is without doubt the strongest accurate hitter golf has ever known. There are few par-5 holes in the country that he cannot reach in two. Yet so fine is his control of tee shots that he hits across the corners of the most dangerous of dogleg holes, taking short cuts no other player could risk. At 5 feet 10 inches and 177 pounds, Palmer isn't big, but he is wonderfully coordinated, with the build of a football halfback. He has large shoulders, outsized arms and broad, strong hands. His waist is small (32), and his hips so narrow that he is constantly hitch, hitch, hitching at his pants as he walks. His legs are developed on the proportion of his shoulders, as solid and tough as a mountain climber's.

All of his powerful physique comes into play when he hits a drive, the ball leaving the tee like lead shot booming from a shotgun. The ball carries 280 yards or so, to a chorus of sound from the gallery that is predictable, instinctive and irrepressible, a long drawn-out OOOHH. Having hit, Palmer is down the fairway at a pace that leaves followers panting behind. He is literally racing to the next shot. His stride as much as says, "You think that shot was something? Watch this one." His every action lets a gallery see how he feels. On good days his face has a constant about-to-smile quality, though he rarely smiles. On bad days he walks even faster, deep-set brown eyes glowering furiously, as if the unfortunate turn of events was a personal insult demanding immediate redress. In such circumstances he gives up hitching at his pants, and his shirttail comes out in back, a flapping banner of dismay. Palmer doesn't play a golf course, he assaults it. "He goes right for the throat of a course," says fellow professional Jerry Barber, "and then he shakes it to death."

The cigarette so frequently in his lips (half a pack a round) is not merely dropped as Palmer prepares for a shot, it is flung aside. He looks at the green, plans his shot quickly and then turns to stare at the crowd if it is not his turn to hit. "People think I am looking for somebody," he says. "I'm not. I just don't want to look at the shot again. I've learned that the way I see it the first time is the best way for me to play it."

The way Palmer sees a shot is usually right at the hole. "Why hit a conservative shot?" he says. "When you miss it you are in just as much trouble as when you miss a bold one." Part of Palmer's boldness stems from the knowledge that he is one of the finest get-out-of-trouble players in the business. "Some players are wonderful hitters of the ball, but they can't figure out ways to get out of trouble," says Palmer. "Eighty

GOOD HUMORED Palmer, at age 19, smiles with Harvie Ward, who had just tied the course record at Oak Hill Country Club; Palmer was eliminated in the match play event's third round.

BETTMANN/GETTY IMAGES

percent of the time there is a way. You just have to know how to look for it." He feels, properly, that what would be a gamble for others is a relatively safe shot for him. Palmer's attitude doesn't change when he reaches the green. He crouches his body into a question mark, stands slightly pigeon-toed and knock-kneed and hits the ball hard at the hole. He may play an entire tournament without leaving a single putt short of the hole. "I putt like I did when I was a kid," he says. "When you're a kid you're not scared of anything."

He has a monumental desire for victory. "I don't care if it's bridge (at which he bids too high, of course), gin rummy or anything else," he says, "I can't be casual about losing." He refuses to admit defeat. "I always think I have a chance to win until winning is absolutely impossible," says Palmer. Yet when defeat does come, Palmer appears to accept it almost stoically. The British were as much impressed with his graciousness after what must have been a deeply disappointing loss in the British Open as they were with his excellent play.

Since his attitudes won't let him be diffident or resigned about a single shot, Palmer exhorts Palmer all around a golf course, and the gallery can listen in. Thus, at a recent tournament:

After a missed putt: "Fool!"

An approach left short (a sin to Palmer comparable to homicide): "Come on, stupid."

Another short approach: "You're nothing but an old maid!"

A hooked tee shot: "Damn!"

A badly hooked tee shot: "Damn, damn, damn!"

All of which is accompanied by a rapping of the offending club against the turf, an outraged stomping up the fairway and facial grimaces worthy of a wrestler. This is not temper, for the expressive Palmer conquered his temper years ago when his father saw him throw a club in a junior tournament and threatened to end his golf career forever. Nor is it showmanship, because the words are meant for Palmer, not for the gallery. It is straightforward annoyance with an inadequate golf shot, and Palmer has no brief for inadequacy anywhere. But he is a showman, too. He enjoys rising to an occasion so much that you might almost suspect him of playing poorly in early rounds of tournaments just to set up his dramatic finishes. Such finishes get attention, and since he was a small boy he has thrived on attention.

Arnold Palmer is the son of Milfred (Deacon) Palmer, a no-nonsense kind of native of the Pennsylvania coal and steel valleys, who in 1921 became the greenkeeper at the new nine-hole Latrobe Country Club some 30 miles east of Pittsburgh. When the Depression hit the area he was made the club professional, too, "until things got brighter." "Apparently," he now says, "they never did."

Arnold, the first of four Palmer children, was playing golf at five, breaking 100 at seven and constantly harassing his father or anyone else within earshot by shouting "watch me, watch me, watch me" before swinging at the ball. When there was nobody around to watch, Arnold would indulge in an almost prophetic child's fantasy, coming up to a putt and announcing into a make-believe microphone: "Arnold Palmer is lining up his putt here on the 72nd hole at St. Andrews, ladies and gentlemen. He pauses. The gallery is quiet. He hits it. It's in! He's won the British Open!" For hole after hole this would continue.

Deacon Palmer's golf training of his prescient son was piecemeal, five or 10 minutes at a time sandwiched between curing the slice of a steel executive and checking the damp third green for fungus. Perhaps because it was so casual, young Arnold grew up with an unwavering interest in the game, instead of learning to hate it as he might have done if the training had been more rigorous. In spite of the brevity of the sessions, the elder Palmer got a precept across to his son that was outright golfing heresy. "Swing as hard as you want," Deacon Palmer said. "I was swinging so hard I'd lose my balance on every drive, and sometimes both feet would come off the ground," recalls Palmer.

People indignantly or curiously asked his father why he was letting his boy swing like that. "He'll balance himself better when he gets older, and he'll hit the ball hard, too," Deacon predicted. Palmer is sure the muscles-first approach is what has made him the golfer he is today. "Too many players learn a controlled swing first, then try to increase their distance and they can't," he says. "As a result, a lot of players don't hit the ball hard enough, and never will."

> "I putt like I did when I was a kid," Palmer says. "When you're a kid you're not scared of anything."

Young Palmer practiced what he was taught so hard that his father was forced to fire him as caddie master when he was 13 because Arnold kept locking up the golf shop and going out to hit drives. Yet, in the time he did spend inside his father's shop, he learned the mechanics of golf equipment, knowledge that has contributed much to his game. He began refinishing the heads of his driver and three-wood (the only woods he carries) a dull black and taking off the brand name so that nothing on the top of the club could disrupt his concentration. He also learned to rebuild clubs to suit him. Even now he reshapes the heads of his woods himself and experiments with new sets of irons more than any other touring pro.

In a way, Palmer is still dependent on his father, to whom he returns for help when anything goes wrong with his swing. Until recently their friendly matches with each other were very close, with the Deacon often having the upper hand. "I think he'd rather beat me than win a tournament," Deacon Palmer said last year. "He'd come home after winning a tournament and I'd knock him off and tell him to go out and win a bigger one."

By the time he was a student at Latrobe High School, Arnold

THE FAMILY LINE Deacon Palmer, playing above, went against orthodoxy by teaching his son to swing hard and learn balance later, producing a stroke that was unusual and powerful.

OPPOSITE: ROGERS PHOTO ARCHIVE/GETTY IMAGES
JOHN DOMINIS/THE LIFE PICTURE COLLECTION/GETTY IMAGES

Palmer had decided he was going to be a golf professional, and tended to be lax about studies that didn't seem to further that ambition. Sandlot football, which his family frowned upon, kept him in doctors' offices, and lunch-hour pool, which his school frowned upon, kept him in spending money. He was, he says, "a hell-raiser." At Wake Forest College, which he attended on a golf scholarship, he continued his easy living while also becoming one of the best intercollegiate golfers of his time. Then, in 1950, his senior year, his best friend and fellow golfer Buddy Worsham was killed in an automobile accident after offering to drive Arnold to a dance at Duke. A shaken Palmer quit school, the first time his confident approach to life was jarred.

Enlisting in the Coast Guard, Palmer came out in 1954. Later that year he won his first major title, the National Amateur Championship. Shortly after that, during a Labor Day tournament at Shawnee-on-Delaware, Pa., he met Winifred Walzer, 19, the daughter of a Bethlehem, Pa. canned goods company president. "Arnie was a pretty fast operator," remembers Winnie. Four days after he met her, he proposed to the snub-nosed brunette. They were married a few weeks later.

The following January, Palmer started on the professional tour. "I was ambitious as hell," he says of that first year. "It took money to play in the big tournaments, and the only way I could get the money was by winning it."

But he was playing too boldly and suffering from faults that still bother him at times, primarily weak short iron and wedge shots and occasionally hooked woods. He won only $8,000 in 1955, improved steadily until 1958, when his first Masters victory helped him become the leading money winner of the year with $42,600, then dropped off to $32,460 in 1959. The reason for the decline in winnings was ragged putting. When his putting improved in early 1960, Arnold Palmer had arrived as golf's best.

Now it was "watch me, watch me, watch me" for real.

In one tournament last fall he hit a ball into a nearly impossible lie behind a green. "Palmer is in a little trouble here on 15," said a true-to-life radio announcer in a hushed voice that carried out over the tense, silent gallery. "You can tell them Arnold Palmer is in an awful lot of trouble," said Palmer, his forelock bobbing impishly. The gallery laughed. Then, stage set, he hit the ball two inches from the hole. It

was more than a golf shot, it was a magnificent production. "You might as well face it: Arnie is a ham," said Winnie Palmer when told of the shot. Ham or not, Palmer's uncanny ability to sink winning shots has given birth to a new verb in golfing circles—"to Palmer." When a pro tells of sinking a chip shot, for example, he may say, "I Palmered it right in." The word carries an implication of 1) laudable skill and 2) a smidgen of good fortune.

Because he Palmered in so many golf shots, Arnold's three-bedroom white ranch house overlooking his father's course near Latrobe has become the focal point of a hectic sporting enterprise.

Winnie is in charge of the two blonde Palmer girls, Peggy, 4, and Amy, 2, and the telephone. The telephone is the most demanding. Its ringing marks the stream of requests for Palmer's services, some blithely brash, others pleasingly promising. The ones he and Mark McCormack, his business manager and lawyer, accept amount to a cornucopia of lucrative enterprises that pushed Palmer's 1960 income up to $190,000. Last year Palmer played 22 exhibitions at an average of $1,500 each. A company brought out a line of golf clothes in his name; another started an Arnold Palmer golf shoe. He collects royalties on sales of his Wilson golf clubs, endorses Munsingwear golf shirts, L&M cigarettes and Heinz catsup. He is part owner of an electric golf car company. His weekly newspaper column, The Palmer Method, is becoming a daily piece, and his first golf instructional book is being published. Among projects that he may become associated with soon are a chain of golf courses, a variety of golf-practice devices, golf toys and even an Arnold Palmer bug repellent.

Palmer's popularity has even enabled him to exercise directly his yen for showmanship. He has appeared on *What's My Line?* (they guessed it), *Masquerade Party* (so did they) and *The Perry Como Show.* His schedule is as crowded as a first tee on Sunday. In one nine-day period last summer he played golf or held business meetings successively in Connecticut, Long Island, upstate New York, New Jersey, Massachusetts, Ohio, Illinois, Missouri and Indiana. During this time he shot three 66s and three 68s.

Only the pursuit of his latest hobby, flying, has allowed him to keep up the frantic pace that success has brought. Palmer is an accomplished but as yet unlicensed pilot. Taking a commercial pilot along in the twin-engine aircraft he likes to rent, he has in recent months logged 200 hours of flying time, some of it in weather that would have grounded a duck. He often invites the touring pros to fly with him, but gets only one taker, fellow Pennsylvanian Art Wall.

His enthusiasm for flying is bounded by no speed limits. At Pensacola this spring Palmer badgered a pilot from the Navy's Blue Angels stunt team to take him up in a two-seater F-Nine-F jet so that he could fly it. "We're 50 feet off the ground and the pilot says, 'All yours, Arnie,'" Palmer recalled before a grillful of listeners at a tournament last fall. "The first thing I know, I've got her in a 6G turn. We gain some altitude, and the pilot tells me how to roll her. I give her a little flip, and there we go, corkscrewing across Florida." And there goes Palmer, too, setting down his Seagram's V.O. on the rocks, waving his arms with more verve than he ever puts into the description of a golf shot. "We get up to 20,000 feet and the pilot says, 'Point her straight down and I'll pull her out.' So I stick her nose at the beach and down we go at 650 mph. We pulled out at 50 feet."

GAME FACE
Palmer was expressive as he circled the course, openly lamenting miscues, relishing his greatest feats, and giving a show to those in his galleries.

BETTMANN/GETTY IMAGES

Palmer ends his story with less zeal. The Navy pilot, whom he got to know well, was killed when the same plane crashed the day after Arnie won the Masters last April.

There are other things Palmer does which such a sports celebrity could think twice about, i.e., working with power tools, playing baseball and football with local kids, Indian wrestling and crossing Fifth Avenue against the light. Considering his daring on a golf course, all this is understandable. But there is a streak of western Pennsylvania conservatism in him, too. Winnie is not permitted to wear fingernail polish, dyed hair is a Palmer anathema, and when he built his house three years ago it was too small because he insisted on paying for it with cash. Since then a den, a garage and a full finished basement have been added. On the less conservative side, he has owned 17 automobiles in five years, from a watermelon Ford to a white Cadillac, and he is a lavish tipper.

To "Palmer" carries the implication of 1) laudable skill and 2) a smidgen of good fortune.

Arnold Palmer's intense desire to win every tournament he plays has not diminished with successive victories but remains as firm as ever. He is now especially eager to win the British Open, and talks of trying to capture the Open of every country that holds such an event. (There are 24 of them.) "Money is not as important to me as championships," he has said. In a sense, Palmer is an amateur in a professional sport. The business sidelines that have developed as he prospered frankly bore him. He has shrugged off his success in his matter-of-fact fashion, enjoying it but hardly reveling in it. Recently he went to a high school football game in Huntington, W. Va. "Nobody will know me here," he said happily to a friend, a little bit of the old hell-raiser's spirit in his voice. "We'll walk around down by the end zone and if anybody comes over I'll say I'm a scout from Wake Forest and you say you're a scout from Maryland."

Minutes later a youngster in a football uniform came running up. Arnold Palmer put on his best scout-from-Wake-Forest look. "Yes, son?" he said importantly. "Excuse me," said the boy, holding out a crumpled popcorn bag, "but would you autograph this for me, Mr. Palmer?"

The Covers

Arnie graced SI's front page fifteen times

June 13, 1960

January 9, 1961

July 15, 1963

June 15, 1964

April 5, 1965

June 12, 1967

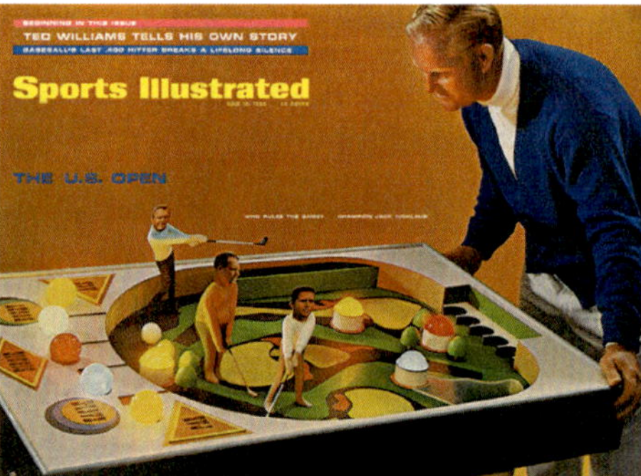

June 10, 1968

September 1, 1969

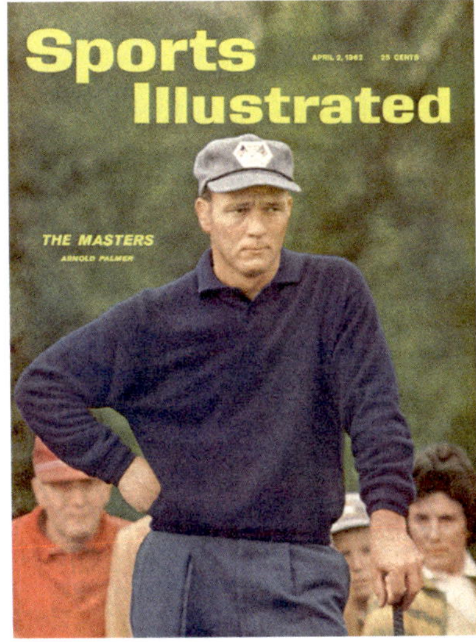

April 2, 1962

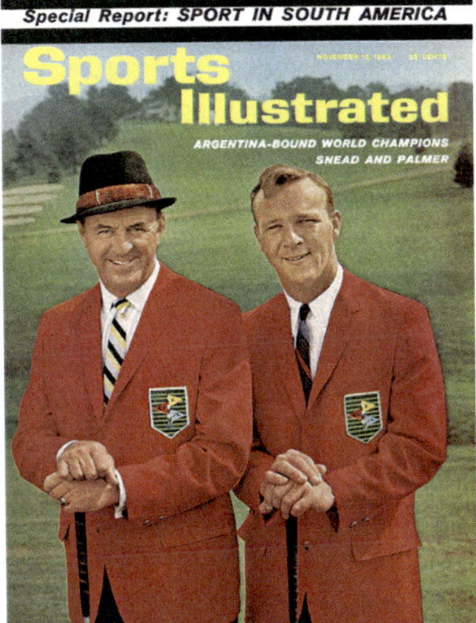

November 12, 1962

July 26, 1965

April 4, 1966

March 6, 1967

June 1, 1970

October 3, 2016

Sports Illustrated

Editorial Director Christian Stone
Creative Director Christopher Hercik
Director of Photography
Marguerite Schropp Lucarelli

Arnold Palmer: The King 1929–2016

Editor Bill Syken
Designer Mimi Park
Photo Editors Robert Conway, Rachel Hatch
Writers Michael Bamberger, Ray Cave, John Garrity, Dan Jenkins, Ian O'Connor, Rick Reilly
Copy Editors Katherine Pradt, Nancy Ramsey
Writer-Reporter Jeremy Fuchs
Editorial Production David Sloan, Richard Shaffer

TIME INC. BOOKS
Publisher Margot Schupf
Associate Publisher Allison Devlin
Vice President, Finance Terri Lombardi
Vice President, Marketing Jeremy Biloon
Executive Director, Marketing Services Carol Pittard
Director, Brand Marketing Jean Kennedy
Finance Director Kevin Harrington
Assistant General Counsel Andrew Goldberg
Assistant Director, Production Susan Chodakiewicz
Senior Manager, Category Marketing Bryan Christian
Brand Manager Katherine Barnet
Associate Prepress Manager Alex Voznesenskiy
Project Manager Hillary Leary

Editorial Director Kostya Kennedy
Creative Director Gary Stewart
Director of Photography Christina Lieberman
Editorial Operations Director Jamie Roth Major
Senior Editor Alyssa Smith
Assistant Art Director Anne-Michelle Gallero
Copy Chief Rina Bander
Assistant Managing Editor Gina Scauzillo
Assistant Editor Courtney Mifsud
Special thanks: Nicole Fisher, Kristina Jutzi, Seniqua Koger, Kate Roncinske

Published by Sports Illustrated Books, an imprint of Time Inc. Books
225 Liberty Street • New York, NY 10281

We welcome your comments and suggestions about Sports Illustrated Books. Please write to us at: Sports Illustrated Books, Attention: Book Editors, P.O. Box 62310, Tampa, FL 33662-2310. If you would like to order any of our hardcover Collector's Edition books, please call us at 800-327-6388, Monday through Friday, 7 a.m.–9 p.m. Central Time.

MARCO GARCIA/PGA/GETTY IMAGES

Made in the USA
Middletown, DE
19 November 2016